OH DEAR,

THE BABY IS HERE!

The ABC's of Caring for Your Newborn

DEON EDWARDS

Dedication

Thank you to my mom and dad, Novelette and Elias, for serving as models of great parents.

To my hubby, Wayne, who fills my days with much laughter on our journey together. Thank you for always nudging and encouraging me to take the next step of faith into the unknown.

Asher, Whitney and Melodie are the inspiration for this work. It's through your growth from infancy to young adulthood that I've learned the essential lessons of life—love, giving and sacrifice.

Thank you to my siblings and the very large network of family and friends that have always been and will forever be MY VILLAGE.

Oh Dear, the Baby Is Here!!!

"Aaaaaaay!, Aaaaaay!." *The shrill of her cry pierced the room as we stood awestruck by the sight and sound of another miracle of life. My face was flushed with tears, my body ached and my heart was entrapped in a web of emotions. With each thump I felt joy, nervousness, relief, uncertainty, exhilaration and anxiety. I whispered a prayer, "Thank you, Lord."*

Two days quickly passed and it was time to take her home. The cards, flowers, gift basket from the hospital room were all packed and we said goodbye to the hospital staff. Our bundle of joy was swaddled cozily by my side as the car drove slowly down the streets towards our home. I stared into her eyes and thought, "She is surely a gift, my pride, my joy and also---my new BIG RESPONSIBILITY. As we rocked with the motion of the car, I thought, "How will I be able to do it without the nurses? Where do I start? Panic gripped me tightly and the questions darted, "When should I feed her? What if she cries all night? How do I know when she's wet? How do I change her diapers? Does she need a bath now? How do I wash her hair? Should I?" I thought I was fully prepared for this new experience, but there were still so many questions that needed to be answered, NOW.

Every day babies are born to first-time moms and dads around the world. Many experience a plethora of emotions as they excitedly embrace the joys of parenthood while bracing for the challenges it may bring.

Oh Dear, the Baby Is Here is a guide to help alleviate some of the anxieties and doubts about caring for your newborn. It addresses frequently asked questions by new parents and serves as an inner voice of experience walking with you through the first few months of parenthood. Helpful information, tips and remedies recommended by doctors and experienced parents will make caring for your newborn more manageable than you imagined. Here we go!

Frequently Asked Questions by New Moms and Dads

What You Need to Know Before It All Begins

Okay, It's Time to Dive In!

It's Time to Bathe My Baby

Dressing My Baby 43

Preparation for the "What Ifs" 48

What You Need to Know Before It All Begins

Preparing for Your New Roles

Are we ready?

Anxieties experienced by new parents often result from feeling unprepared to handle the new responsibility of a newborn baby. Many expecting moms and dads often wonder if they will be able to fulfill their new roles. Will I be able to provide for my baby's needs? How will I know what to do? How much will this change my life? Relax. Everything will be okay and you will be wonderful parents. As you begin this journey, make a commitment to do the following:

1. Embrace your new role.
2. Be willing to learn.
3. Parent together; it takes teamwork.
4. Ask for help.
5. Spend time with your baby.
6. Enjoy and capture every moment.
7. Be willing to make sacrifices.

Will parenting affect our relationship?

Unfortunately, some relationships don't survive the responsibilities of parenting due to the strain it can potentially place on intimacy, especially if there were challenges prior to the baby's arrival. Caring for the baby coupled with work and other responsibilities all bear heavily upon your relationship and can easily weaken it. Therefore, commitment to spending quality time together is also important as you adjust to your new role as parents. Be careful not to shrug your partner's needs to the side by placing all of your energy and attention on the newborn. Instead, carve out specific days and times during each week when you and your partner will talk, listen to each other, engage in fun activities and enjoy the simple things that bring you joy as a couple. Learning how to share your time between your partner and the baby is a process, but it is necessary to maintaining your relationship and creating a healthy environment for your child.

Before the baby arrives, spend time discussing the effects a newborn may have on your relationship. Make a list of the responsibilities your newborn will bring and discuss what role each person will play (i.e. washing baby's clothes, going to the supermarket, late night feedings, etc.). Don't assume that your partner knows your expectations. Take time to discuss them and where there are disagreements, be sure to resolve them.

If you are no longer in an intimate relationship with your baby's mother or father at the time of birth, maturity and self-sacrifice will be required of both adults to set aside personal needs and prioritize your child's well-being. Never underestimate the significant impact a healthy, loving environment has on a child's physical, social and emotional health.

How does mom prepare for her new role?

Expecting parents are sometimes so preoccupied preparing for their new addition that they forget about themselves. Never forget YOU. Mothers preparing to give birth are advised to prioritize self-care given the physical changes that occur with child birth. Here are some helpful tips for both moms and dads.

Spend time with yourself

- *Spend time alone.* Listen to your thoughts. If you are feeling anxious, think positive and consider possible solutions or answers to questions you may have. Be okay with not knowing or being in control of everything.
- *Schedule spa treatments.* Some spas provide massages especially for pregnant mothers and fathers. If a spa is not affordable, take long warm (not hot) bubble baths.
- *Exercise* - Prepare physically and mentally by incorporating exercise routines in your daily schedule such as yoga, walking and other low impact activities.
- *Journal.* Maintaining a journal to capture your thoughts and feelings can be very therapeutic because expression helps to relieve our fears and anxieties.
- *Listen to soothing music.*
- *Read a good book.* A really juicy novel can provide a great escape and balance to your day.
- *Look beautiful.* Expecting mothers should visit the salon, style your hair, get a full manicure and pedicure. Looking beautiful usually helps one feel beautiful.
- *Spend time with your spouse/partner.* Go out to dinner or take a weekend getaway. These moments before the baby arrives are especially helpful because they provide opportunities for you to talk about the changes that will occur and clarify the role each will play in various areas.

- *Make arrangements for additional help.* The first two weeks can be emotionally, mentally and physically exhausting. Dad may schedule a week's vacation or seek paid help, if affordable. Don't be shy to ask family and friends to assist with daily responsibilities such as cooking, cleaning and washing. Create a schedule and ask for close relatives to volunteer one day or even half day to assist you in any way they can.

Self-Care AFTER Childbirth

Family and friends are often so busy helping new parents prepare for the arrival of their newborn that they sometimes forget to caution new moms about some of the physical and emotional discomforts that may result from childbirth. Some new moms are unprepared and alarmed by what they experience after giving birth simply because no one informed them. While experiences after giving birth may vary, below are some common aches and irritations new mothers have experienced and how to prepare for them.

Vaginal birth - Moms who have vaginal deliveries will experience soreness in the vagina. For some mothers, severe discomfort can result from tearing or an episiotomy in the vagina during natural childbirth. To reduce swelling, apply a soft cold cloth and ice pack daily. In a few days swelling and soreness will decrease. When leaving the hospital, be sure to ask for a squirt bottle to clean the vaginal area. After bathroom use, squirt water in the vaginal area instead of wiping to reduce irritation of the area. After birth, bleeding continues for several days, which will necessitate wearing a super absorbent sanitary napkin. Some women also experience constipation and should avoid straining when toileting. Stool softeners are very helpful in addressing constipation.

Remember, experiences vary but one thing is sure—your body will heal. That's the miracle of birth.

Cesarean section - For moms who give birth through a cesarean section, the after birth experience is significantly different from natural birth. Cesarean section is an abdominal surgery and requires tender care of your body thereafter. During the healing process, new moms will need assistance from family and friends in attending to the needs of her newborn and doing basic household tasks. When taking showers, be careful not to wet the area of the incision. If you notice any seepage (i.e. blood, pus) from the incision, notify your doctor immediately. Mothers are advised not to lift anything heavier than the newborn until they receive clearance from the doctor on the first postpartum visit. Again, as you go through the process, remember the one thing that is sure--your body heals with time. That's the miracle of birth.

Postpartum depression (PPD) – New moms are often unaware that childbirth results in significant changes or imbalances in your hormones. As a result, a large majority of women experience "baby blues" during the first few weeks after childbirth. Don't feel ashamed, guilty or embarrassed. Share your feelings with experienced moms and you will be surprised to hear similar stories. While "baby blues" fade after a few weeks, some women experience more severe blues that last longer. Some common symptoms of PPD include: unreasonable fear and worry, excessive crying, feeling incompetent and inadequate, feeling you're not a good mom, not bonding with the baby, frequent mood swings, irritability, social withdrawal, loss of appetite, insomnia, fatigue, thoughts of harming yourself or your baby. If you are feeling sad for an extended period of time, don't be ashamed to share how you are feeling with your partner and doctor. Sometimes new moms are unaware of PPD and are reluctant to share because they feel something is wrong and they might be the only one experiencing these emotions. If "baby blues" are experienced beyond two weeks, is getting worse and your emotional state prevents you from caring for your baby, contact your doctor. Remember, never be afraid to share what you are feeling.

While the cases are rare, some dads also experience postpartum depression. Common factors affecting PPD in men include hormonal changes after the pregnancy, feeling disconnected from mom and baby, and sleep deprivation. Again, please share what you are feeling.

"Don't forget about YOU!"

How's the baby? Can I see the baby? Is the baby sleeping well? Is the baby eating? The baby, the baby, the baby. While it is expected that friends and family will be focused on the baby, YOU cannot afford to forget about YOU. Your physical, mental and emotional health is critical to your effectiveness in caring for your newborn. Proper self-care improves your daily mood, overcomes "baby blues," postpartum depression and all of the challenges being a first-time parent may bring.

1. **Make time for yourself.** You will never *find* the time for you, you have to intentionally **make** the time. In other words, carve out sacred minutes (30 mins., 45 mins.) of each day just for you. Start each morning right! Brush your teeth, meditate, comb your hair, put on fresh clothes, a little make up and eat breakfast. Go outdoors and get some fresh air, even if it's just 5-10 minutes. If baby is still sleeping, read a book, magazine, browse social media, anything that makes you feel

energized and in touch with the world around you. Listen to music, dance a little. If you are completely healed, engage in a short exercise routine. Remember, you don't need a lot of time to do the small things that will contribute to your physical and emotional health.

2. **Prioritize** – Each morning you awake, there will be many competing priorities—housework, loads of laundry, grocery shopping, baby's needs and other tasks. Remember, a newborn changes your routines, your schedule and limits your ability to accomplish all that you usually do. That's your new reality! It's okay if the house is not spotless. It's okay if all the laundry is not done in one day. Pace yourself. Don't try to do everything. Pick THREE by prioritizing the three most important tasks to be completed for each day and try to accomplish them without sacrificing the sacred time set aside for yourself. If some things fall by the wayside, it's okay because they will.

3. **Stay hydrated** – Drinking lots of water is healthy for all mothers, whether or not you are breastfeeding. Utilize water bottles that keep water or juices cold for extended periods of time. This will minimize the task of having to go to the refrigerator each time, which is one reason why moms don't drink as much as they should.

4. **Eat. Eat. Eat.** - Be sure to eat three meals a day to maintain your health and energy. If you are breastfeeding, it is definitely a necessity. Also, adding more vegetables to your diet will help in shedding additional pounds gained during pregnancy. Between feeding, changing, nursing baby, laundry and other housework, eating easily slips to the end of the TO DO list and before you know it, your energy wanes. Maintain a basket of fruits and healthy snacks on your table or

countertop to ensure you are continually refueling throughout the day.

5. *Limit cooking dinner* – I know it sounds odd, but cooking can consume your time and energy. Consider other ways to ensure a healthy dinner without doing it yourself every day. Ask a family member. Contract a family or friend at a reasonable price to cook select meals twice per week. You never know, family and friends might be surprisingly excited and willing to lend a hand in that way. On the days you have to cook, ask for assistance. Be sure your partner is home or ask a relative or friend to assist you with the baby while you work in the kitchen. On the weekend, budget for take-out at least one day. Just don't try to do everything as usual. Scale back or you will easily become overwhelmed and miss out on precious time bonding with your newborn.

6. *Pay attention to your body.* If you are experiencing fever, headache, dizziness, speak with your gynecologist immediately. Don't ignore any irregular or uncomfortable feelings. Remember, childbirth is stressful on the body and the recovery period requires your careful attention.

What is dad's role?

Dads often underestimate the importance of their role during this time. What you do or fail to do affects mom's emotional state and the overall experience of welcoming a new addition to your family.

- *Be on time to pick up mom and your newborn from the hospital.* Mothers are usually ready and excited to go home immediately after they are officially released from the hospital. Be ready and waiting.

- *Make mom feel special and loved.* The baby is the center of everyone's attention and affection, but remember that mom still needs to feel loved. It is recommended that couples abstain from sexual intercourse for approximately six to eight weeks following childbirth (vaginal or Caesarean) because a woman's body needs to heal from the trauma of childbirth. Bleeding usually continues for days, the cervix must close and any tearing that may occur must be healed. Intercourse can disrupt this healing process and result in hemorrhaging or infection in the uterus. However, there are so many other creative ways to express your love for her.

  - Purchase a bouquet of flowers or a basket of fruit/ snacks when she arrives from the hospital.
  - Place love notes or "post its" on the side table, kitchen counter and other prominent places around the house as often as you can. These small reminders are appreciated.
  - Tell her you love her. She needs to hear it.
  - Give her lots of spontaneous hugs and kisses.
  - Make arrangements for babysitting and take her out on a date night.

- *Bond with your baby.* Feed your baby. Change your baby. Comfort your baby. Take every opportunity to be hands on with your baby and spend time getting to know him or her. Don't relegate these tasks to mom only. Many dads are surprised at how easy caring for a newborn becomes as they continue to practice. More importantly, they gain so much more time bonding with their newborns.
- *Share house chores and baby-related tasks.* Taking care of a newborn plus doing the usual chores (i.e. washing dishes,

cleaning, laundry, etc.) can become overwhelming very quickly. Be sure to share the load, if you don't already do so. If you are working full days each week, make arrangements for someone to assist with the daily chores. Consider laundry service for at least one month. Contract a high school or college student to assist after school.

- **Take time off from work, if you can.** The first two weeks at home are important as you become familiar with your new role and also help mom to adjust. Taking time off from work helps in making the necessary adjustment to parenting. Time is one of the most valuable gifts a dad can give to his newborn. Paid paternity leave is offered by some city and state agencies or private companies. Inquire in advance and file the necessary paperwork.

Preparation Before Baby's Arrival

The key to reducing the anxiety of waiting for your newborn to arrive is planning and preparation. Preparation begins six to eight weeks before the baby is scheduled to be born. The last thing you need is an early delivery and being unprepared for the untimely arrival of your newborn. Forget superstitions. Carefully save receipts of all purchases in case returns are necessary.

Some new parents may ask, How do I prepare? What should I purchase? Preparation begins with packing mom's bag for her stay in the hospital and purchasing the basic necessities for the new addition. Do not overwhelm yourself by purchasing everything at once. Take one step at a time.

Preparing a special place for your newborn

One of the first tasks in preparing for your new arrival is to designate specific spaces in the home for him or her.

- *Determine where the baby will sleep.* Is there a designated room or will your newborn sleep in your room for the first 3-6 months? Some parents prefer the baby sleeps in their room, while other parents are quite comfortable with the newborn in his or her own room with a baby monitor. The next question is whether to purchase a crib, bassinet or both. Some parents prefer a bassinet as it is small, cozy and can usually be placed in the parent's bedroom. However, keep in mind that the baby quickly outgrows the bassinet in less than six months and will have to be replaced with a crib. It is also an additional expense since a crib is still needed. Do what is affordable or most comfortable for you. However, baby should never sleep in the parents' bed, no matter how great the temptation to have baby close to you.
- *Purchase baby furniture or designate drawers in existing furniture specifically for baby items.* Select a place where baby's clothes, blankets, bibs, socks, towels and other items will be kept. Organization of these items in a designated area helps to make your first week more manageable.

What are the essentials in selecting a pediatrician?

Your pediatrician will be your partner and guide in taking care of your baby during the first few years. Carefully select a reputable pediatrician at least two months before you're scheduled to give birth.

Tips in making your selection:

- Speak with family, friends, doctors and pediatric nurses for recommendations.
- Choose a pediatrician located close to home.
- Pediatrician should be affiliated with a hospital in close proximity to your home in case of an emergency.
- Check to be sure the pediatrician is covered by your health insurance.
- Meet with the pediatrician and become familiar with his or her style, mannerism and practices.
- Determine if the office hours are convenient for your schedule.
- Ask about the average wait time during office visits, if that's a criterion for you.
- Carefully observe the office environment as your baby will make several visits there.

Where will we deliver our baby?

Traditionally, many couples choose to deliver their babies in a hospital. However, if your pregnancy is low risk, moms and dads have various options including birthing centers or a midwife. Take the time to research these unconventional options as you may find them more suitable for your family. Some insurance companies cover these options, so it is worth the inquiry.

What are the most important items to be purchased before the baby comes home?

First time moms and dads usually feel overwhelmed by the array of items needed for the baby. While it is ideal to purchase all items the baby will use within the first six months (i.e. carriage, swing, etc.), it is not necessary. Focus on the baby's immediate needs and then take it one day at a time. There are also many local programs and community centers that provide some of these basic necessities for newborns. Some pediatric offices provide information on the names and locations of these various centers or organizations. Below is a list of items that should be purchased at least eight weeks before your newborn arrives.

Clothing
- 6 receiving cotton blankets
- 10 undershirts with side snaps
- 10 onesies [size 0-3 months and 3-6 months]
- 7 Socks
- 10 cloth diapers for multiple uses (burp cloth over shoulders)
- 3 mittens to prevent baby from scratching face
- 3 hats to keep head warm
- 7 nightgowns with drawstring (Warm and easy access to diaper)

As family and friends await the arrival of your newborn, everyone is super excited about the adorable outfits displayed in stores and magazines. However, remember that growth is rapid and your tiny newborn will quickly become an infant and toddler. Resist the urge to over purchase and consider the following as you go through those magazine pages and clothing racks:

1. Purchase clothing two-three months larger than the baby's current age. Avoid over purchasing of clothes size 0-3 months, unless your baby is smaller in size due to premature birth. It is better for a baby to be comfortable in a larger sized clothing than to outgrow "just right" sizes.

2. Clothing must be appropriate for the weather during the season of birth. Babies should wear an extra layer of clothes as they tend to lose heat more rapidly than adults. However, avoid too many layers of clothing as babies can develop heat rash.

3. While some clothing are cute, be careful of harsh fabrics. Read tags to ensure clothing is made from 100% cotton.

Bedtime items:
- crib
- bassinet (optional for first three months)
- crib and bassinet mattress pads
- waterproof liners (bassinet and crib)
- 2-4 cotton blankets
- fitted sheet for crib and or bassinet/cradle. [Be sure there is a bassinet or crib prepared for the baby. It is helpful to have baby sleep in your room (not on your bed) in order to hear his or her cry during the night. If the baby is in another room, be sure to purchase a baby monitor. Bassinet or crib should be wrapped with crib sheet and a soft blanket. Avoid the use of pillows as they can cause suffocation].
- 1-2 sleep sacks (optional)
- Humidifier or vaporizer (optional)

Bath time
- small bathtub
- hooded towels
- wash cloths
- baby wipes
- baby soap
- shampoo
- powder with cornstarch (optional)

- gauze [to be used on circumcised penis]
- baby brush and comb
- natural hair oil (check with doctor for recommendations)
- A&D ointment, Desitin or petroleum jelly. [To prevent chafing, any of these ointments or barrier creams can be placed on baby's bottom and around penis or vagina after each diaper change. Also place ointment or petroleum jelly over the foreskin of the circumcised penis and cover with gauze until completely healed].
- newborn diapers [Swaddlers are diapers for newborns and usually include a small opening at the navel to prevent irritation of navel string until it detaches].
- bottle of alcohol (optional) [Soak cotton ball with alcohol or a swab and dab navel, which will help the navel to heal and detach faster. Be careful that alcohol doesn't seep into baby's vagina or penal area. This should be done daily until the navel string is completely detached].

Feeding items
- Bottle nipples [Carefully look at the label to be sure the nipples are for newborns 0-3 months as the size of the nipple hole determines the flow of the milk. The hole should be the smallest for newborns].
- 4 oz. baby bottles [Newborns normally drink between 1 – 2 oz. during the first few weeks. Also, purchase different brands of bottles until you select a system (Avent, Dr. Brown, etc.) that is best suited for your baby.
- bottle sterilizer
- baby water [filtered water made especially for newborns]
- scrubbing brush for bottles
- Milk storage bags or bottles
- small bibs [size of bibs vary according to baby's age]

- Breast pump, if breastfeeding. (Inquire about wireless, hands-free breast pumps that can be worn under clothing)

Other important items
- baby bag [a large bag is suitable for newborns. As baby grows older, smaller bags are sufficient.]
- nasal aspirator
- fingernail clip
- digital thermometer
- Rear facing car seat
- Sun shield for car window
- Mild detergent [It is recommended to iron the baby clothes or wash them to remove all possible germs before use].
- Diaper disposal bin [optional] If not affordable, wrap diapers in small plastic bags before placing in garbage to conceal odor].
- Baby monitor
- Night light for late night feedings or diaper changes
- Sling or wrap (optional)

Essential items for mom
- Breast pads
- Nursing brassiere (provides opening for easier access to the breast)
- Nightgown or loungewear (button down for easier opening to breast)

What does mom need for the hospital?
Be ready to go at any time. A small travel bag with the following items should be packed and easily accessible at least six weeks before the baby's delivery date.

- *nightgowns or pajamas*
- *Bed slippers*
- *maternity brassieres*
- *lanolin ointment or lotion for nipples [if breastfeeding]*
- *washcloth*
- *toothbrush*
- *underwear*
- *body lotion (avoid lotions with fragrance)*
- *feminine pads*
- *cosmetics (when you look beautiful, you will feel it)*

Baby is Ready to Go Home

The day your baby leaves the hospital is one of the most memorable moments and should be captured and cherished forever, so be *prepared*.

- Don't forget electronic device for capturing pictures and videos
- Secure car seat in back of the car
- Dad or a designee should be prepared with baby's bag which should include: bibs, diapers, wipes, blanket, an outfit, hat, socks
- Clothing for mom

It's time to head home, and the journey begins!

Okay, It's Time to Dive In!

First Evening at Home with My Newborn

The first few hours at home with your little bundle of joy is when you become fully immersed in the role as parents. It is during these first moments you discover how much you already know and how much you are unsure about. Parental instincts usually kick in and you will do what only seems natural. However, to ensure the best care for your baby, some fundamentals are important to know.

What is the right room temperature?

Keep your baby comfortable by ensuring the temperature in the room is moderate, between 68 and 72 degrees Farenheit. Adjust thermostats and gauges on air conditioners to be sure the baby is neither too hot or cold. Keep baby's bassinet or crib away from vents, which sometimes blow dust particles. If needed, a humidifier is helpful as it allows for better ventilation in the room. On cool days, open windows and allow the baby to breathe in fresh air. Remember, do not overdress your newborn. Babies sometimes cry incessantly due to many unnecessary layers of clothes that leads to increased body temperature and discomfort. During warm months, one layer of clothing is sufficient. During colder months, place two layers of clothing in addition to the coat or jacket when venturing outdoors.

Am I holding my baby correctly?

When holding your baby, be sure to support the back and neck as muscles are not fully developed. Place the baby over your shoulder and use your right or left hand to support the baby's neck. Place a dry cloth or a small blanket over your shoulder to prevent your baby's face from rubbing against harsh and soiled clothing. The baby may also be positioned in the cup of your arm with the arm serving as support for the back. Do not be afraid to correct other adults who may be holding the baby incorrectly.

Oh my, how do I change my baby?

Frequent changing of the baby's diapers prevents chafing, diaper rashes and other discomforts. Baby diapers should be changed usually every two-three hours, immediately after a bowel movement, before and after nap time, bedtime, and before leaving the house. This is one of the first tasks you will perform as a new mom and dad.

- Lay the baby on the bed or on a changing table. Place the baby on his or her back on a towel or blanket.
- Fold soiled diaper under the baby's bottom and wipe excess feces to prevent it from getting on the sheet or changing pad. Then, slide the soiled diaper from under the baby's bottom and wipe the baby from front to back (particularly girls) with a warm damp cloth. During the first three weeks when the baby's skin is most sensitive, use a soft damp cloth instead of baby wipes. Be sure to clean between the folds of the skin.

To avoid odor, place the soiled diaper in a diaper basket or inside a small plastic bag before placing it in the garbage.

- Pat area dry and to prevent chafing, apply a small amount of A & D ointment or other creams *around* the vaginal and penis area and on the bottom. Do not use powder in the diaper area.

- Holding your baby's ankles, raise your baby's legs and lower body and slide a clean diaper under the bottom with the tabs towards the back.

- If the baby is circumcised, paste a generous amount of A & D on a piece of gauze and place gently on the tip of the penis before closing the diaper.

- Close the diaper by bringing the front flap up and pressing the tape to the Velcro. Make sure not to fasten the diaper either too tightly or too loosely. You should be able to comfortably run two fingers between the diaper and the baby's stomach.

Navel Care

- The baby's umbilical cord stump dries out and falls off on its own usually between one to three weeks. Once the stump falls off, the navel area is exposed and must also heal. Keep the area clean, dry and exposed to air for healing. Monitor for irritation, redness, odor or drainage.

- According to the American Academy of Pediatrics, it is recommended to leave the cord alone and let it dry and fall off on its own. Studies have shown no difference in the infection rate with the use of alcohol. If you choose to use alcohol, dip a swab in 70% alcohol and dab a generous amount on the baby's navel. Continue each day until the navel string detaches.

- Place the diaper fold under the naval. Some newborn diapers include an opening for the naval.

- It is recommended to use side snap undershirts instead of onesies as they do not cover and irritate the healing navel.

How do I know my baby's diaper needs to be changed?

Manufacturers are designing diapers for longer use and some include indicator lines that change colors when diapers are saturated. Some parents determine if diapers are wet simply by squeezing diapers to see if it's swollen. One parent says it feels squishy, which usually means the gel has been activated and if it isn't wet, it feels like dry cotton wool.

Begin Chart.

Keeping track of your baby's activities is an important task for every mom and dad. Tracking helps you to quickly recognize any changes or irregularities in a baby's activities--sleeping hours, feeding times, formula amounts, stool, urine, etc. Tracking also better enables you to inform the pediatrician about your baby's activities and patterns in the event he or she becomes ill. Immediately begin using the chart provided in the appendix. Be sure to complete all information on the chart and remember to be *consistent*. Chart should be used for at least six-eight weeks until you are familiar with the baby's patterns. Many parents also use apps that can hold the newborn's information more easily and stored on your device.

It's sleepy time! What do I need to know?

Newborns tend to be asleep more than they are awake as they sleep about 16 to 18 hours each day. That is normal as sleep is necessary for growth. Unfortunately, SIDS (Sudden Infant Death Syndrome) is one of the leading causes of death among newborns up to about six months and occurs mostly when babies are asleep. When placing your baby in a crib or bassinet, the baby should be positioned on his or her back, according to the American Academy of Pediatrics. The cause of SIDS is not definitive; however, some experts believe it may be the result of less oxygen intake when babies are placed on their stomachs. DO NOT use sleep positioning devices as they are not proven to prevent SIDs and, rather, have been the cause of infant deaths. While moms and dads want to keep their newborns close, it is also **not** recommended that babies sleep in the bed with parents. Your repositioning during the night, unaware of the baby's presence, can result in your rolling on the baby.

Tips to ensure your baby sleeps comfy and safely

- Be sure to remove all pillows and blankets from the crib and bassinet, and always check on the baby frequently when asleep.
- Place the baby on a firm crib mattress. As comfy as they may seem, avoid pillows. Babies can easily burrow their faces in them and breathing becomes challenging. If they are unable to breathe, babies are too young to shift their position.
- Do not keep stuffed and soft toys in the crib because they can be hazardous when the baby is sleeping.
- Keep cribs and bassinets away from vents and other sources of drafts (i.e. air conditioning and heating vents, windows, etc.)

When will my baby sleep through the night?

Newborns tend to sleep between two and four hours during the night as they awake for feeding due to their small stomachs. As they get older and their stomachs grow, they will be able to go longer between feedings and thus will sleep longer during the nights (6 to 8 hours). Some babies may begin sleeping through the night after three months, while others may take longer. *Each baby is different.*

When your baby awakes during the night, various methods can be used to help him or her go back to sleep. Walking, rocking, soft pats on the back, pacifiers, soft soothing music are different ways experienced moms and dads help babies go back to sleep.

Important reminders during the first week

Rest. You will receive many calls and visits from family and friends who are excited to see your new bundle of joy. However, establish a bed time of no later than 10:00 p.m. and when possible, take naps whenever the baby is resting. Remember, you are now operating on the baby's schedule, not yours. So take advantage of every minute of sleep that becomes available.

Eat and Drink. Again, it is so easy to be consumed by the new addition that you forget about yourself. Moms must eat well-balanced meals each day, especially if you are breastfeeding. Breastfeeding moms should also consume large amounts of water in order to produce milk. Lack of meals and liquids during this time can lead to crankiness and reduce your stamina to take care of a newborn. Remember to take prenatal vitamins while breastfeeding to help replenish the nutrients transferred into your breastmilk. Meals high in protein will also help decrease any feelings of lightheadedness and fatigue while nursing your newborn. Don't underestimate the benefits of eating and drinking.

Family and Friends. While everyone wants to hold the new bundle, individuals with colds and flu should avoid holding the newborn as babies are more susceptible to germs. Be sure to lay a soft towel or burp cloth over the shoulder of the adult to protect your baby's face from harsh fabrics or germs . Everyone should use hand sanitizer when entering your home or wash their hands with soap and water. Also, discourage family and friends from kissing the baby on the face as germs and viruses can be transferred to the newborn. Hugs are great and are safe expressions of their love!

It's Time to Feed My Baby

Food is the most essential element of a baby's physical development. It is also the topic that stimulates most discussion among veteran and first-time parents. Some moms choose to breastfeed or formula feed exclusively, while others choose to do both. Studies have provided many reasons why breastfeeding is beneficial both to babies and mothers.

What are the benefits of breastfeeding?
While there have been many advances in the production of baby formulas, a mother's breast milk is the most nutritious and the healthiest choice for a developing infant.

A mother's breast milk is the healthiest food for babies because it is natural and contains all the necessary nutrients needed for a baby's growth. As babies grow and continue to breastfeed, the volume and composition of the milk changes to promote healthy growth. Breast milk is also digested easily and reduces constipation, diarrhea and upset stomach sometimes found in formula-fed babies. Breastfed babies tend to have fewer colds, influenza and less respiratory and ear infections. Some studies found that breastfed babies tend to have less food allergies, skin rashes and eczema. Brain and nerve growth and development of immune systems are other benefits of breast milk.

Mothers also benefit from breastfeeding as it reduces post-partum bleeding and helps to return the uterus to its shape. Breastfeeding also helps mothers lose weight as studies show significant weight loss in women who breastfed during the first year. Many moms find breastfeeding easy and convenient because it's readily available, the temperature of the milk is right, and it's cheaper. Frequent touch and holding of the baby during breastfeeding also develops a strong bond between mother and baby.

Ceriline Smalls, nurse practitioner and lactation specialist, strongly encourages breastfeeding and shares tips for moms who choose to breastfeed.

How is breast milk produced?

The amount of milk each mother produces varies and can be attributed to many factors including frequency of feeding, liquid consumption, etc. However, milk production is driven mainly by supply and demand. The amount of milk the breast produces is also determined by the amount of time spent breastfeeding. It is recommended that breastfeeding or pumping occurs eight to twelve times within 24 hours. The more the baby demands, the more the breast will produce. If supplementing with formula, the breast milk should still be removed from the breast. Smalls advises that failure to remove milk either by breastfeeding or pumping will result in a decrease in milk supply. The body may believe it is making too much milk or the milk is no longer needed. Massaging the breast during feeding or pumping can also help push more milk out of the milk ducts. While you may wish to use both bottle and breast milk, it is recommended that you rely more heavily on the breast instead of the bottle during the first few months.

Breastfeeding necessitates adequate fluid intake and a balanced meal as dehydration and hunger can decrease milk production. It is strongly suggested that the breastfeeding mother consumes large amounts of liquids. In the morning, be sure to drink a large cup of tea in addition to a large glass of water or juice. It is also recommended that mothers drink before and after feeding. To increase milk production, Smalls encourages moms to use a technique called "power pumping," which mimics cluster feeds when breastfeeding. Pump for 20 minutes, rest for 10 minutes; pump for 10 minutes, rest for 10 minutes and pump for another 10 minutes. In one hour your brain will think the infant needs to be fed three times, and your body will naturally produce more milk.

Breast Pumping Machines

For moms returning to work, there are a number of breast pumping machines on the market that are helpful to continue breastfeeding after maternity leave has ended. Breast pumps are electric, battery-operated, manual and even hands-free. Visit local baby stores and even specialty shops and research the cost and function of the various products available. Most health insurance companies now cover the cost of breast pumps so call and inquire.

How should I care for my nipples when breastfeeding?

First-time moms who breastfeed are sometimes afraid to continue when they experience soreness. The number one reason for nipple soreness is poor attachment or latching. Breastfeeding should not be painful. In the initial seconds of feeding, the latch may be uncomfortable, but as the feeding continues it becomes relaxing. During feeding, the brain releases oxytocin, the "love hormone," that makes breastfeeding relaxing and increases the bond between mother and baby. When breastfeeding, remember to switch breasts as your baby's constant pulling on any one breast during feeding can and will cause soreness over time.

Nipples should remain moist at all times. Moisten breasts with over the counter ointments after each feeding and cover nipples with breast pads to prevent exposure to air that causes breasts to crack. It is also important that breastfeeding moms do not allow the breast to become engorged (full, puffy, swollen), which is a direct result of infrequent feeding. Engorgement of the breast can be very painful and the only remedy is releasing the milk from the breast. Breastfeeding requires patience and persistence, but the benefits to both mother and baby are long lasting.

What should I know about baby bottles?

Choosing the right brand of bottles for your baby is not difficult but requires trying different brands before determining the most suitable one for your baby.

Types of Bottles - Bottles are different shapes and sizes. Feeding bottles are made of glass and last long, but they are heavy and tend to be more expensive. Plastic or silicone bottles are hard, lightweight and less expensive. Some bottles are wide, straight or contoured. Bottles are designed in small and large sizes as newborns and older babies consume different amounts of milk. Smaller bottles are typically four ounces and larger bottles eight ounces.

Bottle Nipples - Bottle nipples are designed to ensure the flow of milk is suitable for newborns and older babies. Nipples for newborns provide a slow flow of milk so the baby doesn't drink too much at once. Larger nipples are designed for older babies who are able to swallow more and at a faster pace. Newborns usually consume one to two ounces per feeding while a six-month old consumes six to eight ounces. New parents should also look for bottles with anti-colic nipples, which reduces the amount of air the baby swallows thus reducing or preventing gas. When creating your registry, you may begin with one brand. If your baby works well with that brand, then continue using it. Popular brands include Dr. Browns, Phillips Avent, Tommee Tippee, Comotomo, Medela, etc. Family and friends usually share recommendations or feel free to read reviews of various brands before making your selection.

Cleaning Bottles

Keeping your baby's bottles clean and dry is a daily task. Some parents purchase a sterilizer exclusively for the baby's bottles. However, placing bottles and nipples in soapy hot water for five minutes is also fine. Use a cleaning brush to get into the narrow nooks. Bottles can also be cleaned in a dishwasher. Be sure water is drained from bottles after each wash.

How do I choose the most suitable brand of formula for my baby?

Selecting the formula that is best for your baby is another key decision that may require consultation with your child's pediatrician. Paying careful attention to your baby's response to the select formula is critical to ensuring it is the right choice. Keep in mind that babies respond differently to various formulas and, therefore, choosing the best formula might require trying more than one.

There are three types of formulas--cow's milk, soy(vegan) and specialized formula for premature babies and babies with special needs. Formulas are sold as powder, liquid concentrate or ready-to-feed. Cow's milk is most common and doctors often recommend that parents begin with cow's milk as it's easier to digest. Some parents choose soy as a vegetarian diet is preferred. Hydrolyzed formulas contain broken down cow's milk proteins that make digestion easier for babies. Hydrolyzed formulas are recommended for babies with allergies or are at high risk for developing allergies. Doctors also prescribe specialized formulas for babies with special medical needs.

There are many brands of baby formulas on the market. If you are not breastfeeding or if you are both breast and bottle feeding, then speak with your pediatrician and get recommendations. Some mothers continue using the formula received from the hospital unless the baby has an adverse reaction to it. The formula you choose is simply your preference and continued use is based on your baby's response to it.

Which formula is best--Ready to feed, concentrated, or powder?

Parents choose different formulas for various reasons. Most infant formulas are fortified with iron as they attempt to mimic breast milk. The **Ready to Feed** formula is convenient because it is already prepared; however, it is most expensive. **Concentrated** formulas require adding water to specific ounces of formula. Some parents prefer it because they can mix warm baby water with the concentrated formula to produce a warm bottle. The **powder** is usually the least expensive and is also preferred by some parents.

There are common indicators that your baby cannot tolerate the formula. Diarrhea, severe constipation, vomiting, blood in bowel movement, crying, lack of weight gain, or weight loss are some signs. Carefully observe any changes in your baby and consult your pediatrician immediately.

Should my baby drink warm or cold formula?

It is recommended that the baby's formula is served at room temperature. However, some parents prefer to provide warm milk. Use a bottle warmer or you may stand the prepared bottle in a cup of hot water until warm. Before feeding, shake the bottle and test the temperature of the milk by pouring a small amount on your wrist. **Never feed the baby before determining the temperature of the formula.** Tip: For quick preparation of bottle during the night, store hot water in a thermos. If using concentrated formula, mix the cold refrigerated formula with the warm water from the thermos to make a warm bottle. This is only useful when using concentrated formula as the mix requires half water and half formula. Again, test the temperature of the milk before feeding.

When preparing a bottle using concentrated or powder formula, you may use bottled water prepared specifically for babies. If using tap water, it is recommended to run the water for 15–30 seconds before filling your baby's bottle. Many homes have lead in their plumbing pipes, but running the water for a few seconds allows the standing water in the pipes that may be filled with contaminants to pass. Some parents also strongly recommend boiling the tap water before using it.

How do I position myself and the baby for feeding?

First, find a quiet place and be sure you and your baby are positioned comfortably. Feeding time is a great opportunity for mothers and fathers to bond with their newborns. Make feeding a time to hold your baby close and let him or her feel your touch.

Breastfeeding

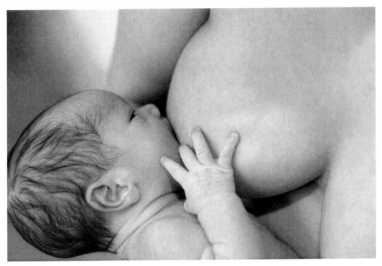

When breastfeeding, place the baby in a comfortable position in the crouch of the arm, cup the baby's head in your hand and bring him or her up to your breast. The nipple should not be placed directly in the baby's mouth as breastmilk is not produced in the nipple. The nipple is like the "straw." When you begin breast-feeding, the nipple should first be aimed to the nose, and when an infant smells the milk the mouth will naturally open wider and the head will tilt back. Hug your baby in towards you to get a deep latch; the chin should be on the breast. Be sure the entire dark area of your breast (areole) is in the baby's mouth. Watch for movement at the side of the baby's face nearest to the ears to determine if your baby has latched on correctly and is pulling the milk. Be sure to switch breasts to prevent soreness and other effects of overuse.

Before leaving the hospital, attend a breastfeeding class, which is usually offered by most hospitals. Join a local breastfeeding support group or browse the internet for instructional videos that may also be very helpful.

Bottle Feeding

When bottle feeding, the body of your baby should be cupped in the corner at the bend of your arm and forearm. Baby should never lay flat, but should be held upright while feeding. Be sure to hold the bottle upright so the formula flows into the baby's mouth. If the bottle is not held upright, air seeps through the nipple and babies can develop gas as a result.

Reminder: Dads must be given the opportunity to bond with their newborns also. If mom is breastfeeding, then during feeding intervals, dad may burp the baby. After feeding, allow dad to hold the baby close for a period of time before laying the baby down.

How often should I feed my baby?

Newborns usually consume between one-two ounces of milk every four hours during the first month. Use the chart (see appendix) after each feeding to record the quantity consumed and the frequency of feeding. Newborns typically nurse for approximately 20 minutes, but may nurse longer as they grow. Be sure to allow adequate time on each breast during feeding. However, if your baby continues to cry uncontrollably after feeding, baby may not be satisfied and may need more feeding time. However, be careful not to overfeed your baby.

How do I burp my baby?

It is best to burp the baby at intervals during feeding. If the baby drinks two ounces of feeding, stop the baby after one ounce and burp. *First position*: Place the baby over your shoulder and gently massage or lightly pat your baby's back area while listening for the burp. Be sure to place a clean burp cloth at all times over your shoulder to prevent the baby's face from rubbing on your clothes. After you hear the burp, you may continue feeding. *Second Position*: Hold baby in sitting position on lap (support neck with hands) and gently tap baby's back until you hear the burp and then resume feeding. If the baby spits up a small amount of feeding, no worries as that's normal.

For how long can I use leftover formula or breast milk?
Formula left at room temperature should not be used after an hour due to the quick buildup of bacteria. Formula that has been prepared can be refrigerated and used up to 24 hours. *Breast milk* can sit at room temperature for up to four hours. Breast milk stored in the refrigerator can last three to four days.

When should my baby be given cereal?
You may begin to feed your baby cereal between four to six months. It is recommended that you mix cereal with warm water and feed your baby from a bowl using the spoon. However, many mothers and grandmothers place a small amount (half teaspoon) of cereal in the baby's formula to thicken and keeps baby satisfied for a longer period of time [not recommended by doctors].

Are pacifiers good for babies?
Pacifiers are used by many parents to help soothe and calm babies. Babies have a natural reflex and urge to suck, so providing a pacifier after your baby's belly is full meets this need. Pacifiers are soothing and can help babies fall asleep, but should be removed as soon as the baby is fast asleep. Pacifiers are also helpful during air travel as it reduces air pressure when an airplane

is taking off and landing. However, some experienced parents and doctors warn against overuse of pacifiers.

It is not recommended to use a pacifier within the first thirty days of breastfeeding as this may cause nipple confusion for your baby. Studies also show that ear infections are likely among babies who frequently use pacifiers. Some parents are concerned about the effect of pacifiers on teeth growth. Parents suggest allowing your baby to self soothe first, and try various ways to comfort your baby to avoid dependence on the pacifier. As your baby grows, use toys and other objects as alternatives to the pacifier. The goal is to begin to reduce the frequency of use after approximately six months.

It's Time to Bathe My Baby

Is it time to give my baby a full bath?
Not yet. Newborn babies should not be immersed in water until the umbilical cord is completely detached. Instead, babies should be wiped or sponged using a damp cloth.

Sometimes new parents are surprised and alarmed because the baby's skin doesn't look like those seen in commercials. Don't freak out. It's okay. Matter of fact, many newborns may have skin irritations, rash, dryness and peeling that result from being in the amniotic fluid for nine months. However, soft skin occurs over time, usually within the first few months.

How do I wash my baby before the first bath?
1. Fill basin with lukewarm water and place on a large flat surface or in an area close to where the baby is laid. Gather all items needed for sponging your newborn (towel, washcloth, diaper, cream/ointment, cotton swab, gauze).
2. Place the baby on a towel on the bed or on the changing table. Do not remove all clothes at the beginning as the baby will be cold. Begin cleaning the baby by wiping the face, beginning with the eyes (wipe from the inner to the outer corners of the eye).
3. Wipe forehead, cheeks, chin and other areas of the face. There is no need for soap yet; lukewarm water is sufficient. Rinse cloth.

4. Remove clothing from baby's upper body.. Gently lift the baby's neck and wipe the back and front parts of the neck. Be sure to get in between the creases. Rinse cloth. Wipe the baby's armpit and move downward to wipe the stomach and back areas. Stop and rinse cloth.

5. Use A&D ointment (avoid oils and lotions) and gently moisturize the baby's upper body. Place a clean undershirt on the baby. It is recommended to use side snap undershirts instead of onesies as they do not cover the healing navel.

6. Remove diapers. For girls, wipe the vaginal area beginning from the front backwards. Never wipe from the back forward as bacteria from feces may be wiped into the vaginal area causing infection. For boys, wipe the penis area and gently wipe the tip of the penis. For newborn boys, after wiping penis, apply a generous amount of A&D ointment on a strip of gauze and place it over the tip of the penis until circumcision is healed. Then apply A&D ointment or Desitin to the area surrounding the penis and on the buttocks to prevent chafing. For girls, apply A&D ointment to the vaginal area and buttocks. Close pampers.

7. Again, be sure to use diapers with navel openings that are made specifically for newborns. This prevents the diaper from rubbing against the umbilical cord stump. This is optional, but some parents help the healing process of the umbilical cord by wetting a cotton swab with alcohol and dabbing the cord daily. However, be sure alcohol remains near the navel area and does not seep into the diaper. The navel area can also be left uncovered to allow the umbilical cord to be exposed to air. Avoid the use of powder during the first three to four weeks. For girls, never place powder in the vaginal area.

8. During winter months, place socks on feet to keep the baby warm.

9. Baby's scalp should be moist at all times to prevent cradle cap, which is flaking of the scalp. Wipe baby's hair with a damp warm rag and gently massage scalp. Place a small amount of baby oil on a soft bristle brush and massage scalp at least twice per week.

When and how do I give my baby a full bath?

Bathing your newborn for the first time is exciting for first-time parents, but it can also be a little nerve-racking. Begin by washing your baby's hair.

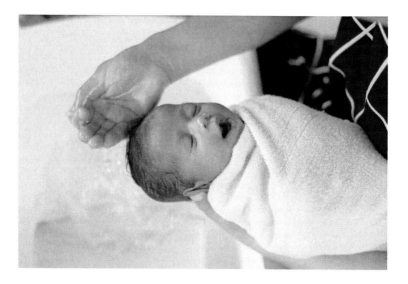

Hair

1. Wash the baby's hair by holding the baby's head in a football cup over the sink or baby tub while the body rests in the bend between your forearm and arm.
2. Wet rag with warm water and a small drop of baby shampoo. Using a rag, lather the entire hair and scalp and then

rinse thoroughly. Be sure to wash away from the baby's face. Stroke backwards to prevent soap and water from seeping into the baby's eyes.

3. Pat hair with a dry towel until it is completely dry.

Body

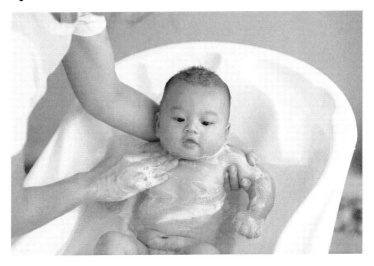

1. Before removing clothing, gather all items needed for the bath (towel, washcloth, diaper, A&D ointment, baby oil, baby powder and clothes).

2. Fill the baby's bath with lukewarm water. Place baby's bath on a large counter or inside the bathtub. Be sure the baby's bathtub is on a flat surface. Some baby bathtubs include a resting pad or sling inside the tub that helps to support the baby and keep them from slipping and sliding. This is very helpful until the baby is old enough to sit upright without your support.

3. Always test the temperature of the water by placing your hand in the water before immersing your baby.

4. Before placing the baby in the bathtub, place the baby on a towel on the bed or on the changing table.

5. Begin cleaning the baby by wiping the face first beginning with the eyes (wipe from the inner to the outer corners of the eye). Then wipe forehead, cheeks, chin, other areas of the face and behind the ears.

6. Remove diaper and all clothing. Place the baby in the bathtub by laying the baby on a tray or resting pad. If you do not have a resting pad, hold the baby in the bend between your arm and forearm. Be sure the baby's back is fully supported by your arm while the other hand is used for washing the baby.

7. Wet washcloth and place a small amount of baby soap on cloth.

8. Wash the baby's body beginning with the neck (front and back), behind the ears, chest, stomach and vaginal or penis area. Turn the baby over and wash the baby's back and buttocks. Wash baby's legs, feet and in between toes. Rinse with warm water.

9. Quickly remove the baby from the bath and wrap in a dry towel. Pat all areas of the baby's body, including behind the ears, until thoroughly dry. Be sure to lift the baby's neck and dry creases.

10. Use baby oil, lotion or continue use of only A&D ointment. Moisturize the baby's entire body using any of the above. Use a generous amount of A&D ointment or cream in the vaginal or penis area to prevent chafing.

11. Place diapers and clothes on.

12. Be sure to discard water from the baby's bath and wash thoroughly for the next bath.

When should lotions and/or powders be used?

Many parents suggest avoiding the use of lotions or powders especially during the first month when the baby's skin is still changing. Natural products such as A&D ointment are recommended to keep the skin moist.

Dressing My Baby

How do I choose the best disposable diapers?

Decisions, decisions, decisions! Choosing the right diaper brand is another important decision first-time parents make as it is essential to your baby's daily comfort. *Cost, softness, absorbency* and *fit* are key factors in selecting the most suitable brand for your newborn.

Some parents prefer cloth diapers as they are cost effective over time and eco-friendly. However, other parents choose the convenience of disposable diapers, some of which are also eco-friendly and biodegradable. Some parents use cloth diapers at home and disposables when going out, so it all boils down to preference.

The size and brand of the diapers you choose depend on your baby's weight and comfort. Disposable diaper sizes vary from one brand to another and usually range in size from newborn – size 6. Different brands of diapers also vary in size as size 1 may be larger in another brand. Also, a brand's weight range usually overlaps: size 2 in one brand will cover kids weighing 12 to 18 pounds; size 3, 16 to 28 pounds and so on. Also, keep in mind that as the size increases, the number of diapers per package decreases while the price may remain the same or even increase. For newborns, it is not recommended to purchase economy size packages as your baby is likely to outgrow the newborn size quickly, unless your baby was born prematurely.

When purchasing, carefully view labels to determine the appropriate size for your baby. Be sure to choose the size that fits your baby snuggly as oversize diapers will result in leakage. Be sure to look for diapers with elastic around the legs that also prevents leaks and fit more snugly. Some disposable diapers have velcro-like fasteners that are more efficient and help to prevent leaks. Diapers with elastic waistbands are also worthy of exploring.

There are a number of brands on the market, so choose what is most comfortable for your baby. Feel free to experiment with different brands during the first month until you have decided which brand you're most satisfied with.

When do I begin using wipes and what types should I purchase?

When choosing wipes, thickness and softness should be considered as it is what is most soothing on your baby's skin. Some wipes are hypoallergenic, while others are sensitive to babies with eczema. It is recommended, however, that wipes be used after the first month as some contain fragrances that may adversely affect your baby's skin.

What size clothing should be purchased for my baby?

Babies grow rapidly. Clothing 0-3 months do not last very long. When purchasing clothing, always buy 2-3 months larger than the baby's current age. Clothes are sized 0-3 months, 3-6 months, 6-9 months, 12 months, 18 months, 24 months and then for toddlers 2T, 4T, etc. If your baby is four months, it is recommended you purchase clothing sized 6-9 months. Also, for families who live in regions with seasons, consider how old the baby will be during each season. If your baby is eight months old in December and you are purchasing clothing for the summer, calculate how old the baby will be by July—15 months old. Therefore, clothing size purchased for the summer should be 18 months. If your baby is above average height and weight, size 24 months may be more suitable. It is helpful to provide friends and families a chart with seasons and sizes, since some gift givers are not parents and sometimes fail to consider these factors when purchasing (see appendix).

Avoid purchasing clothing with strings as they may be potentially hazardous. Purchase clothing with snaps rather than buttons for easy access to diapers. When purchasing pants for your baby, be sure to look for those with adjustable waists. Also, while outfits may be cute, be sure the fabric is 100% cotton as rough fabrics may be harsh on your baby's skin causing some discomfort.

How should my baby be dressed indoors and outdoors?
When dressing your baby, add a second layer. When going out during the cold months, be sure the baby's head and feet are covered. During the winter months, gauge the temperature in the house and be sure to place socks on baby's feet, which traps the heat in the body. During the warm months, only one or two layers of clothing should be placed on the baby as too many layers of clothing may result in heat rash.

How should I care for my baby's clothes?
During the first few weeks, it is recommended to hand wash your baby's clothes using a mild soap or detergent, such as Dreft or Ivory. If using a washing machine, please be sure to wash your baby's clothes separately. Avoid fabric softeners as fragrances may be too harsh for baby's skin.

What should I pack for my baby the first time we're going out?
It is convenient to have a bag for your baby packed at all times. During the first months, a large bag is needed for various items listed below. As baby grows older, a smaller travel bag is sufficient as less items will be needed. Baby's bag should always include these basic necessities when going out for two to four hours:

- 3-4 pampers
- 2 outfits

- case of wipes
- A&D ointment
- 2-3 burp cloths
- 3 bibs
- receiving blanket
- small thermos (optional: to make warm bottle using concentrated formula)
- pacifier (if used)
- 2 bottles of formula or pumped breast milk
- insulated bottle holder

Depending how long you will be away from home, make two bottles and place them in a thermal bag (sold in stores) in addition to a ready-to-feed can. Small cans of ready-to-feed formulas are sold for your convenience. You may also carry a small bottle of cool baby's water.

What should I consider when purchasing a car seat?

Keeping your baby safe starts with the car ride home from the hospital. Purchasing a safe, comfortable car seat requires knowledge of some basic information. First, choose between an *infant carrier* or a *convertible* car seat. Infant carriers are only for a limited time, up to 12 months. However, they are convenient because they can be detached from the base and carried with you or snapped into a stroller that is compatible. Convertible seats last until your baby is a toddler and is more cost effective. However, they cannot be removed from the car, which can be inconvenient especially when babies are sleeping and you don't want to wake them. For safety, car seat must have a five-point harness (shoulder straps, waist straps, and a strap between the legs that meet in the middle) with cushioned head and neck support for comfort and protection. Infant car seats should always face the rear of the car. Before purchasing a car seat, measure the back seat of your car to be sure the base of the baby's car seat will fit. Check if your car has a LATCH system that consists of built-in straps and hook to secure your baby's car seat without use of a seatbelt. Car seats have expiration dates usually between 5 and 7 years, so be sure to check the expiration date if your car seat has been used.

Now that we've covered the basics of caring for your baby, let us discuss some unpredictable events you may encounter that caused first-time parents some anxiety and even alarm. Every baby is different, so your experiences may not be the same as others. However, it is wise to be familiar with and prepared to respond in the event the unexpected occurs.

Preparation for the "What Ifs"

What if my baby is crying uncontrollably?
A baby's constant cry may be the result of hunger, a wet diaper, griping or your baby may simply want to be held. There are several ways you can comfort a crying baby. First, be sure your baby is not wet, tired, hungry or has a temperature. Sometimes a baby may cry uncontrollably because of griping or an ear infection. Babies are also very uncomfortable when they are teething. Don't worry. There are many ways to try to calm your baby as persistent crying can be frustrating for moms and dads who are running out of remedies as the cries grow louder and longer.

- If your baby is experiencing wakefulness, rock the baby in your arms, a bassinet, glider or rocking chair. Slow steady motions often soothe the baby until he or she goes off to sleep.
- Walk around the house with your baby.
- Stand up and repeatedly bend your knees to provide motion.
- Stroke the baby's back or tummy.
- Place the baby in a soft blanket and swaddle.
- Turn on soft music or an appliance that makes a sound (i.e. dryer, vacuum).
- Walk the baby in a carriage or stroller.
- For older babies, the motion of a car ride around the block often rocks the baby to sleep.

The key is to keep trying. While one method may not lead to the desired outcome, try another method. You may also try the same strategy at another time as it may work the second time.

What if my baby is colicky?

According to the Academy of American Pediatrics (AAP), about one-fifth of all babies will develop colic, which can begin during the first month of birth. A colicky baby repeatedly cries for extended periods of time with occurrences commonly in the evenings and night. Some indicators of colic are the baby's incessant crying, passing gas and kicking of legs while crying. Colicky babies can cause moms and dads to feel both helpless and frustrated. Therefore, it is important to ask for help when you feel you are burning out. While there is no specific cause for colic, some parents warn against overfeeding the baby as this can lead to discomfort in the stomach. Other parents suggest the baby be properly burped after each feeding. Signs of colic may also stem from the type of formula your baby is fed or even the diet of the breastfeeding mom. Swaddling and rocking are ways to soothe a colicky baby and over-the-counter medicines may also be a remedy.

How should my baby's poo look?

During the first few days after birth, babies normally pass meconium, a dark green and sticky tar-like texture. Don't panic. Meconium is made up of substances your baby ingested while in the uterus and is an indicator that your baby's bowels are functioning normally. After your baby begins to receive breastmilk or formula, meconium will be pushed out of the system and the poo will gradually change. Baby's poo will become greenish and then yellowish in color. The color of the baby's poo may vary as it depends on the formula and what the breastfeeding mom eats.

Baby's poo should be loose in texture and may be grainy at times, but should be passed easily. Babies who are formula-fed may pass stool that is thicker in texture. The frequency of a baby's poo varies as newborns may poo from one to four times per day. However, If your baby shows discomfort when pooping and stool is hard and dry, baby may be constipated. If no bowel movement occurs in more than two days, the baby becomes uncomfortable or the abdomen is swollen, contact your pediatrician. Use the chart (see appendix) to record the frequency of your baby's bowel movements.

What should I do if my baby is constipated?

Most babies usually suffer with a bout of constipation at some point within the first twelve months and even beyond. Constipation often results from the types of food your baby consumes. At other times, it may be an adverse effect of the formula, the food consumed by the breastfeeding mom or even dehydration.

If your baby becomes constipated, massage the stomach right below the navel to loosen any firmness felt there. To loosen the firmness in the stomach area, lay the baby on his or her back and pedal feet in a forward motion. Doctors also recommend a glycerin suppository sold over the counter that will stimulate the rectum and allow stool to pass. However, suppositories should not be used frequently. If your baby is not yet eating table food and often becomes constipated, consult your pediatrician and consider changing the formula or tracking the food consumed by mom, if breastfeeding.

As your baby grows and is ready for table foods, be careful to begin with foods that are less likely to cause constipation. While applesauce, rice cereal and bananas are among the first starters for a baby, too much rice cereal may lead to constipation. When constipation occurs in babies who are eating solids, consider other alternatives such as fruits and vegetables that include pears and broccoli. Experienced parents recommend pureed prunes, pears and apricots in your baby's diet to keep the bowels loose.

What if my baby has diarrhea?

Babies may experience diarrhea as a result of a viral, bacterial, ear infection, or after a course of antibiotics. The American Academy of Pediatrics (AAP) recommends that babies not be given fruit juice before six months as diarrhea may be caused from too much fruit juice or sweetened drinks. Diarrhea may also be caused by formulas not completely mixed or simply by something the baby ate.

Keeping your baby hydrated when diarrhea and vomiting occurs is important as severe dehydration may necessitate hospital care where intravenous fluids (IV) are given. Don't worry if your baby experiences loss of appetite; just be sure to keep baby hydrated because appetite usually returns within one to three days. If your baby is not vomiting, continue with breastfeeding or formula. If vomiting is frequent, consult your doctor who may suggest pediatric electrolyte solutions that can be purchased at the local supermarket or pharmacy. Electrolyte solutions are sold in various flavors that may appeal to your baby's taste.

Diarrhea may also cause your baby's bottom to become irritated, so be sure to change diapers frequently and gently apply cream after each change.

What if my baby is griping?

If your baby is crying uncontrollably, clenching the fists and passing gas, it is possible your baby is griping. Baby gas is not uncommon and is a result of an underdeveloped digestive system as it occurs mostly in newborns. Gas causes the baby's stomach to be bloated and leads to pain or irritation. Gas may be caused by the baby gulping down too much milk at once or sucking in too much air from a nipple with a slow flow.

Gripe water is often used to soothe pain and other discomfort resulting from gas. Gripe water can be purchased over the counter at your local pharmacy. It includes dill, fennel and ginger that may help to relieve gas, colic and other stomach discomfort.

What if my baby has an ear infection?

An ear infection is an inflammation of the middle ear that is usually caused by bacteria when fluid builds up behind the eardrum. Ear infection in babies and young children are common, especially after a cold, flu, sore throat or other upper respiratory infection. Indicators of an ear infection may include fussiness, crying, tugging at the ear, sleeplessness, fever, and a loss of appetite. If you notice these signs, consult a doctor immediately. Don't worry. Babies usually get better within a few days as doctors may prescribe antibiotic or over-the-counter pain relievers such as acetaminophen, ibuprofen or ear drops. Be sure your baby drinks lots of fluids and gets rest.

What should I expect when my baby is teething?

Excited first-time moms and dads wait expectantly for the first sign of that little budding tooth between five and seven months. However, some babies teethe earlier and even later. The question is, how do I know my baby is teething? What are the indicators? Teething babies drool excessively and they tend to bite down on any surface, including fingers and mommy's breast to relieve the pressure under the gums that is caused by a budding tooth. The tooth pushing through the gum also causes inflammation of the gum, which can be intensely painful for some babies. The discomfort of the gums causes some babies to be irritable and some may lose their appetite. While debatable, some mothers insist that diarrhea and low grade fever are also symptoms of teething.

Soothing remedies for teething babies may include a teething ring, which is rubbery and can scratch baby's gums. Some parents give their babies cold, firm items that include a frozen bagel or a cold rag with cubes of ice tightly wrapped inside. Parents also purchase teething biscuits that work well before any tooth pops out. When all else fails, moms and dads offer their fingers as firm surfaces your little ones can nibble on for relief. Consult your doctor for recommendations of over-the-counter medicines such as Baby Tylenol and Baby Orajel.

What if my baby has diaper rash?

Diaper rashes are caused by leaving a wet or dirty diaper on too long. Rashes are also the result of diarrhea, an allergic reaction to a diaper or detergent, yeast or bacterial infection, or allergic reaction to antibiotics. If your baby develops a rash, use plain water on the baby's bottom and pat instead of rubbing sore skin. Avoid wipes with fragrances or alcohol; use a soft washcloth instead. Always pat the area dry before putting on a new diaper. To prevent rash, many parents frequently use a cream or ointment during each diaper change that contains zinc oxide or petroleum jelly.

Rashes heal faster when exposed to air. So, as often as possible, let your baby go without a diaper. Doctors recommend changing the brand of diapers or choosing a different detergent (hypoallergenic). If after two or three days of treatment the rash worsens or doesn't change, pay attention to signs that may include fever, yellowish bumps, reddish rash or if your baby seems sluggish. Consult your pediatrician immediately as antibiotics or antifungal treatment may be needed.

What if my baby has eczema?

Some babies may develop eczema also known as atopic dermatitis. For some babies, eczema is hereditary while for others it may result from switching from breastmilk to formula or from formula to solid foods. It may be caused by some soaps, shampoos or detergents. Long, frequent baths can cause your baby's skin to become extremely dry. Eczema is a red, scaly rash that can develop behind the ears, on the neck, legs or arms. Areas of the baby's skin can become thick, hard and irritable. The itchy rash is uncomfortable for babies and causes them to scratch. To handle eczema, it is important to keep your baby's fingers clipped and covered with mittens to prevent damage to the skin from constant scratching.

To prevent dryness of skin, bathe your baby less frequently and use mild soaps. After each bath, while the baby is damp, lubricate the skin with doctor recommended creams and lotions for eczema. Keep air in the home moist by using a humidifier. When washing your baby's clothes, use mild detergents and avoid fabric softeners. Dress the baby in soft, cotton fabrics and avoid wool. Carefully monitor your baby's diet as food sometimes causes a flare up or worsening of eczema. Consult your physician for prescribed creams to manage your child's eczema if it persists over time.

What if my baby has a fever?

Babies usually develop fevers, especially in the winter season. A fever is an indication that the baby's body is fighting an infection. The American Academy of Pediatrics (AAP) suggests that a normal body temperature for a healthy baby is between 97 and 100.3 degrees Fahrenheit. When a baby's temperature is high, he or she may become uncomfortable and unwilling to eat, drink, or even sleep. If your baby feels unusually warm, first remove any extra layer of clothing and then take the temperature.

How to take your baby's temperature - Using a digital thermometer, place it under the baby's underarm and hold for approximately 60 seconds. Remove the thermometer and check the temperature. Digital thermometers can also be used in the rectum, which doctors recommend for babies 0-3 months for more accurate reading. Wash the tip of the rectal thermometer with soap and water or wipe with alcohol. Place your baby on the tummy or on the back lifting the legs towards the chest. Spread the buttocks and insert the bulb of the thermometer about an inch into the rectum or until the tip of the thermometer cannot be seen. Hold the thermometer steady until it beeps, then remove and read the temperature. If the temperature is over 100 degrees, the baby has a fever.

Using lukewarm water, sponge baby's entire body wiping especially under the arms. Cool water is also helpful in reducing the baby's body temperature. If your baby's temperature remains above 100.3 degrees Fahrenheit, doctors normally recommend an infant acetaminophen or ibuprofen (if 6 months or older) to bring down the temperature. Follow the instructions of your doctor to ensure the correct dosage is given to your baby, and always use a measuring device. If the fever is reduced after the medication but increases again, consult your doctor as antibiotics may be needed to help fight the infection that may be the cause of the fever.

Febrile seizures - Fevers sometimes cause febrile seizures in babies between five months and age five. Indicators of a febrile seizure may include eyes rolled back, jerking and stiffening of body, drooling or vomiting. It may be terrifying for a parent to watch; however, babies usually quickly recover from febrile seizures within hours. If your baby experiences a febrile seizure, remain calm. Place your baby on the bed or ground on his or her side to prevent choking. Loosen any clothing around the baby's neck or head and watch carefully for 3 to 5 minutes. If convulsions do not stop after five minutes, call 911 immediately. If seizure stops within five minutes, give your baby an ibuprofen or acetaminophen to reduce the fever. Be sure to schedule an appointment with your pediatrician to determine the cause of the seizure.

What if my baby has a stuffy nose?

Nasal congestion is commonly caused by a cold, breathing in dry air, smoke, pollutants or allergies. Keep the air in your home moist by using a humidifier or vaporizer. Clean carpets of pet hair and avoid smoking inside your home. If your baby is congested, a warm bath helps to clear the nasal passageway. Squeeze one or two drops of saline nose drops in each nostril to loosen dried mucus. Use an aspirator and pull excess mucus from the baby's nose. Squeeze aspirator and insert in baby's nose, release aspirator while in the nose for suctioning.

It's okay to be prepared for the "what Ifs," but remember that parenting is like a box of chocolate, you never know what you will experience.

Do's and Don'ts:

Tips from Moms and Dads

Parenting is a beautiful journey filled with many new learning experiences at every phase of your baby's life. Wisdom in parenting is gained through trial and error, new discoveries and listening to some of the Do's and Don'ts like those shared by experienced moms and dads. Some may be questionable while others are helpful, so you decide.

Don'ts

- Don't refuse help. Take the offers of help from family and friends.
- Don't purchase too many "newborn" sizes unless your baby is born prematurely and is smaller in size.
- Don't buy too many *expensive* clothes. Babies don't go out enough to wear them all and will outgrow them quickly.
- Don't refuse new or slightly worn clothes from family and friends. Excited parents usually purchase too many clothes and are often left with many unused outfits.

- Don't purchase a bottle warmer. Use a thermos instead, especially if using concentrated formulas. Mix half and half. Just be sure to test the temperature of the formula on the back of your hand BEFORE feeding.
- Don't purchase an expensive stroller if your weekly activities don't usually require frequent use of one.
- Don't panic every time your baby cries. Be okay with hearing your baby cry until you are able to meet his or her need.
- Don't overfeed your baby in order to pacify him or her. Every cry doesn't mean your baby is hungry. Sometimes your baby might just want to be held or played with.
- Don't wake the baby just for feeding; it's not necessary. Wait until he or she awakes.
- Don't allow your baby to set his or her own bedtime. Train your baby to go to sleep at a specific time each night.
- Don't hold your baby constantly. Your baby will grow accustomed to always being held, and it will be difficult to place him or her down for any period of time.
- Don't always feed your baby warm milk. In case of an emergency, when only room temperature milk is available, your baby may not like it.
- Don't be afraid to use a pacifier; just avoid overuse.
- Don't place toys or stuffed animals in the crib as it's a safety hazard.
- Don't forget to cut your baby's nails. Babies' long, sharp nails can scratch their lovely faces if not clipped frequently.
- Don't forget to pack a pajama when out late at relatives' or friends' home with your baby. Before you leave, change the baby into the pajamas so when you arrive home, just lay him or her in bed.
- Don't argue in front of your baby. As young as they are, babies can sense negative emotions.

Do's

- Give your baby a long warm bath. It is relaxing and helps babies fall asleep faster.
- Sleep slacks are awesome and safer than blankets. Babies also sleep longer in them.
- If you want your baby to go to sleep at 8:00 p.m., then the entire house has to feel and sound like bedtime. Speak softly, turn down the lights, radio and television.
- Sing and talk to your baby. Your voice becomes familiar to your baby and language comprehension begins.
- Purchase a *convertible* car seat that grows with the baby and avoid purchasing more than one car seat.
- Purchase an infant car seat that lasts one year, but can be detached from the base and carried with you. Avoids waking baby.

Conclusion

Parenting is an adventure, so don't be afraid of the journey. Mistakes often result in new learning and you will eventually become more comfortable and confident in your role as the baby grows.

Time is golden and can never be regained once it passes. So, capture and treasure each stage, each day, each experience, each moment. Developing a bond with your baby is a process that is worth the investment of your time and attention because its impact is long lasting. Never allow the responsibility of providing for your baby to displace the time spent hugging, kissing, playing and making your baby feel loved. As your infant grows, be sure to savor those moments and the joy each brings.

Give your child the gift of a healthy home. The environment and experiences we create for our children frames their self-perception, their worldview and helps shape the adults they will ultimately become. Every child needs and deserves a peaceful, loving and nurturing home where they are praised, accepted and have the freedom to express their thoughts and feelings. "Children Learn What They Live," is a profoundly thought-provoking and inspiring poem by Dorothy Nolte. Her wisdom provides insight on the impact a parent's words and actions can have on a child's social and emotional well-being. Children don't always remember what you gave them, but they do remember how you made them feel.

The role of parenting is probably the most important role in one's lifetime. Moms and dads have the awesome responsibility of nurturing and developing a human being from infancy to adulthood. That is no easy feat. However, parenting is not done independently or in isolation, but rather within a village of grandparents, aunts, uncles, cousins, neighbors, teachers and many others who love and care for both you and your children. Take advantage of all the help that is offered and gratefully embrace the individuals who willingly extend their time, attention and resources to help raise your child.

Parenting will become overwhelming at times, but when all else fails, do as many parents have often done----PRAY. "A Parent's Prayer" is a reminder of our common fears, hopes and dreams and our inability to control some of the outcomes. However, wisdom dictates that we do all we can, and those small, sincere prayers will take care of the rest.

Embark with excitement on this new journey of parenting. Many have done it well and so will you.

Children Learn What They Live

by
Dorothy Nolte

If children live with criticism, they learn to condemn.

If children live with hostility, they learn to fight.

If children live with ridicule, they learn to be shy.

If children live with shame, they learn to feel guilty.

If children live with encouragement, they learn confidence.

If children live with tolerance, they learn to be patient.

If children live with praise, they learn to appreciate.

If children live with acceptance, they learn to love.

If children live with approval, they learn to like themselves.

If children live with honesty, they learn truthfulness.

If children live with security,

they learn to have faith in themselves and others.

If children live with friendliness,

they learn the world is a nice place in which to live.

A Parent's Prayer
author unknown

Heavenly Father, make me a better parent
Teach me to understand my children, to listen patiently to what they have to say, and to answer all their questions kindly.
Keep me from interrupting them or contradicting them.
Make me as courteous to them as I would have them be to me.
Forbid that I should ever laugh at their mistakes, or resort to shame or ridicule when they displease me.
May I never punish them for my own selfish satisfaction or to show my power.
Let me not tempt my child to lie or steal. And guide me hour by hour that I may demonstrate by all I say and do that honesty produces happiness.
Reduce, I pray, the meanness in me. And when I am out of sorts, help me, O Lord, to hold my tongue.
May I ever be mindful that my children are children and I should not expect of them the judgment of adults.
Let me not rob them of the opportunity to wait on themselves and to make decisions.
Bless me with the bigness to grant them all their reasonable requests, and the courage to deny them privileges I know will do them harm.
Make me fair and just and kind.
And fit me, O Lord, to be loved and respected and imitated by my children.

Bibliography

American Academy of Pediatrics; Hill. David L. Hill, Altmann, Tanya; *Caring for Your Baby and Young Child: Birth to Age Five,* Bantam 2009 [7th edition 2019]

Eisenberg, Arlene, Murkoff Heidi. E., Hathaway, Sandee E. BSN: *What to Expect When You're Expecting.* Workman Publishing Co. 1989, 1996 [5th edition 2016]

Krieger, Liz. "First days at home with your baby." Babycenter.com. Babycenter. 30 October 2018

Micco, Nicci and Harris. "Picking the Best Newborn Baby Bottle."Parents.com. Parents. Updated 22 March 2021

Rowlee, Chris and Alvarez, Mandy."Pacifier Use: The Good, The Bad & How to Use Them Wisely." Babysparks.com. Health & Nutrition. 21 August, 2017

Tracking Newborn's Functions

Date	Time	Stool Color/Texture	Bottle Feeding Ounces	Breastfeeding	
				Time on Left Breast	*Time on Right Breast*
July 6	*10:06*	*Light green/beady*	*2 oz.*	*15*	*10*

Determining Size of Clothing for Purchase

Age of the baby + Age of baby during the season for clothing – purchase 3 months larger

Example: If you are purchasing summer clothing for the baby in March, consider the current age of the baby and how old he/she will be in July (summer). Purchase clothing 2-3 three months larger than the age of the baby in the season for which the clothing is being purchased (i.e. July-August).

Month When Clothing is Purchase / Age of Baby	Month Clothing to Be Worn / Age of baby		Recommended purchase size
March / 3 months	July	7 months	6-9 months
August / 6 months	January	11 months	9-12 months **OR** 2T (depending on size of the baby)

Average clothing sizes used by most manufacturers
0-3 months
3-6 months
6-9 months
9-12 months
12 months
18 months
24 months
2T
3T
4T 5T